The Harlem
Renaissance

Essential Events

THE HARLEM
RENAISSANCE

BY DEANN HERRINGSHAW

Content Consultant
Regennia N. Williams
associate professor, Department of History
Cleveland State University

ABDO
Publishing Company

CREDITS

Published by ABDO Publishing Company, 8000 West 78th Street, Edina, Minnesota 55439. Copyright © 2012 by Abdo Consulting Group, Inc. International copyrights reserved in all countries. No part of this book may be reproduced in any form without written permission from the publisher. The Essential Library™ is a trademark and logo of ABDO Publishing Company.

Printed in the United States of America, North Mankato, Minnesota
062011
092011

Editor: Mari Kesselring
Copy Editor: Rebecca Rowell
Cover Design: Kazuko Collins
Interior Design and Production: Marie Tupy

Library of Congress Cataloging-in-Publication Data
Herringshaw, DeAnn, 1962-
  The Harlem Renaissance / by DeAnn Herringshaw.
    p. cm. -- (Essential events)
  Includes bibliographical references.
  ISBN 978-1-61783-101-0
  1. Harlem Renaissance--Juvenile literature. 2. African American arts--New York (State)--New York--20th century--Juvenile literature. I. Title.
  NX512.3.A35H47 2011
  700.89'9607307471--dc22
                                        2011015336

TABLE OF CONTENTS

The Renaissance Casino and Ballroom in Harlem

THE TWO HARLEMS

New York City's Harlem neighborhood was an exciting place in the 1920s. It was an African-American community where many intellectuals, writers, artists, and musicians had come to live and do their creative work. Creativity abounded in Harlem. New ideas about what it meant to be African American were inspiring a wealth of literature that in turn inspired art, music, fashion, and community life. This outpouring of creativity made Harlem the center of African-American culture during the 1920s. Leaders in Harlem recognized this was a new birth—a renaissance—of African-American spirit and identity. This important era came to be called the Harlem Renaissance.

Although the Harlem Renaissance was an African-American cultural phenomenon, it soon caught the interest of many white New Yorkers. In the 1920s, most white Americans were ignorant about African-American culture. Segregation kept the races from mixing socially. Laws kept the races from intermarrying. Bigotry kept many light-skinned people believing they were superior to dark-skinned people. But when white people discovered Harlem's exhilarating nightlife, they wanted to get in on the fun.

HARLEM NIGHTS

Harlem after dark was full of stimulating sights and sounds. For outsiders, especially white people who would never want to live there, visiting Harlem

Not in
Our Neighborhood

Many people in Harlem did not like white people infiltrating their neighborhood, treating their culture as if it were created for white people's enjoyment. Prominent Harlem writer Langston Hughes wrote in his autobiography, *The Big Sea*, that resentment toward whites was growing in the black community: "Nor did ordinary Negroes like the growing influx of whites toward Harlem after sundown, flooding the little cabarets and bars where formerly only colored people laughed and sang, and where now the strangers were given the best ringside tables to sit and stare at the Negro customers—like amusing animals in a zoo."[1]

on a Saturday night was an exotic adventure. It gave them a chance to see and hear the best jazz and blues musicians in the world, watch talented dancers, and immerse themselves in a lively atmosphere. It was unlike anything white society offered.

The jazz and blues styles of music were created by African Americans, but the art forms quickly became all the rage in mainstream US culture. This new music gained attention around the world. Since hearing music live was the best way to experience it, white people came to Harlem. In order to capitalize on Americans' appetite for these musical experiences, dozens of nightclubs opened up in Harlem in an area known as Jungle Alley.

PROHIBITION

It may not have been coincidence that the Harlem Renaissance took place during the years of Prohibition, which lasted from 1920 to 1933. During Prohibition, it was illegal to make, sell, or transport any alcoholic beverage in the United States. After the law prohibiting alcohol was passed, liquor stores and bars closed immediately. But, that did not stop people from drinking alcohol.

All over the United States, people opened underground bars. They sold homemade alcohol, called hooch, or bootleg liquor that had been smuggled in from Canada or overseas. These secret bars were called speakeasies because people had to speak quietly about them. Still, law enforcement officers found out about them. They conducted raids on these secret bars and nightclubs and took people to jail. But the police almost never raided Harlem. This helped to make Harlem's many bars, nightclubs, and cabarets into wildly popular nightspots in the 1920s. The most famous were the Cotton Club, Connie's Inn, and Small's Paradise.

The Jazz Age

The 1920s, also known as the Roaring Twenties and the Jazz Age, was a time when people were looking for fun and new experiences. After World War I (1914–1918), many people wanted to throw off old ways of thinking and doing things. They were tired of old-fashioned hairstyles, clothing, and music. Women, who had been restricted by society the most, bobbed their hair, put on makeup, and wore short skirts. To scandalize the older generations even further, young people started listening to jazz music. Jazz was new and exciting; it became the symbol of the 1920s.

Officials pour illegal liquor into the sewer after a raid.

The Cotton Club

The swankiest and most prestigious nightclub in Harlem was the Cotton Club. It was opened in 1923 by a white gangster named Owney "The Killer" Madden, who got his nickname for committing manslaughter. Madden hired only the most talented black performers and attracted the wealthiest patrons. He also employed ex-boxers as bouncers and guards, who made sure only certain types of people got inside. Although the performers were almost all African

Americans, only whites were allowed to sit in the audience. To add to the separation between the races, the Cotton Club often put on elaborate jungle- or plantation-themed spectacles. This reinforced stereotypes of African Americans as savages or slaves.

SMALL'S PARADISE

Another of Jungle Alley's most popular hotspots was Small's Paradise. This was an integrated nightclub owned by African-American Edwin Smalls. Small's Paradise featured top-notch musical talent and spectacular floor shows. All the performers were black, but the audience was both black and white. Small's Paradise was also famous for its dancing waiters who performed the Charleston while bringing trays of food to the customers. When Small's Paradise opened its doors in 1925, Smalls threw an extravagant party. Nearly 1,500 people showed up. It remained the most prestigious interracial club for many years.

Edwin Smalls

Before Edwin Smalls became a famous night-club operator, he was an elevator operator. He descended from Captain Robert Smalls, a South Carolina congressman who was a former slave and a captain in the Union navy during the American Civil War (1861–1865). Smalls opened Small's Paradise in the autumn of 1925. It was the biggest career step of his life. Although he had been running his own Harlem nightclub—the Sugar Cane Club—since 1917, Small's Paradise was much more elaborate. Smalls intended to attract not only local clientele, but also white people who wanted a more authentic Harlem experience—one where white and black people mingled.

The Savoy Ballroom

Opened on March 12, 1926, the Savoy Ballroom was another integrated nightspot, but it was not a nightclub—it was a place to dance. Known as the "The Home of Happy Feet," its huge dance floor was the birthplace of many new dance steps.[2] The Lindy, also known as the jitterbug, was one dance African Americans at the Savoy invented in 1928. Two house bands took turns playing for the dancing patrons. When one band finished a set, the other band took over. Music never stopped at the Savoy.

The Other Harlem

Not everyone who lived in Harlem could

The Renaissance Casino and Ballroom

The Renaissance Casino and Ballroom was true to the spirit of the Harlem Renaissance. It existed to serve the people who lived in the community and celebrate the achievements of African Americans—artists, workers, writers, and sportsmen. Local people went there to dance to the music of world famous entertainers and socialize with one another. The Renaissance Casino and Ballroom rejected establishments such as the Cotton Club, which rejected the African-American community by enforcing segregation.

The Renaissance Casino and Ballroom outshone the bigoted Cotton Club in many ways, but one of the most exciting things about it was its all-black championship basketball team, the Rens. The Rens would play basketball on the dance floor while the bands changed. These athletes toured the United States and endured continual racism, but according to former National Basketball Association player Kareem Abdul-Jabbar, "they helped spread the gospel of the Harlem Renaissance."[3]

afford to enjoy the nightlife of big clubs and dance halls. In fact, many did not have enough money to pay their rent. Though scores of Harlem's apartment buildings were run-down, rent there was higher than in white New York neighborhoods. Because African-American workers were paid less than whites who did the same job, coming up with rent money each month could be difficult. If Harlem residents could not pay their rent, they were in danger of eviction—being put out on the streets. One creative way they found to raise rent money quickly was to throw a rent party.

Rent parties happened in people's apartments all over Harlem, especially on Saturday nights. Whoever was throwing the rent party would send out invitations to friends and neighbors. Then, they would clear out their furniture to make room for dancing. They would charge a small fee—from a dime to

The Tree of Hope

The Tree of Hope was a lucky wishing tree that grew in Harlem near a nightclub called Connie's Inn. Musicians and actors gathered around this elm tree to perform for club managers, hoping to get hired in one of Harlem's many clubs. Legend had it that rubbing the tree would bring good luck.

The Tree of Hope was cut down in 1934 when the city widened the street. Fortunately, one large piece of the trunk was saved and now holds an honored place at the Apollo Theater in Harlem, where performers still rub the wood for good luck before going onstage.

Conrad Immerman

The owner of Connie's Inn, Conrad Immerman was a German immigrant who made his fortune selling bootleg liquor. When he decided to open a nightclub in Harlem, he hired African-American artists and craftsmen to design and build the interior decor. Connie's Inn was an elegant club, showcasing the best African-American talent without reinforcing stereotypes, but only white patrons were allowed in the audience. Immerman, though less bigoted than many white establishment owners in Harlem, still did not think that white customers would want to sit near black people and mix with them on an equal level socially.

50¢—and provide food, music, and alcohol and light their rooms with red or blue lights. Rent parties were not for spectators. They were for people who lived in Harlem.

Saturday nights in Harlem were full of good times for rich and poor alike, but the Harlem Renaissance was about much more than just jazz and the jitterbug. Although it lasted only about a decade, from approximately 1920 to 1930, the Harlem Renaissance would make a powerful impact on the United States.

Dancers at the Savoy Ballroom in Harlem

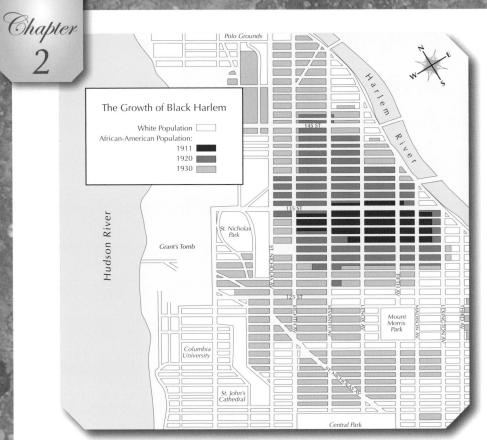

The Harlem neighborhood was a small area in New York City.

From Haarlem
to Harlem

he Harlem neighborhood in the 1920s
occupied about two square miles (3.22 sq km)
of northern Manhattan in New York City. Its
boundaries were not rigid, but the general area was
bordered by the Harlem and East Rivers on the east

• 16 •

and northeast, Saint Nicholas Avenue on the west, and extended from 114th Street on the south to 156th Street on the north.

Harlem: A History

Before there was a New York City or a Harlem, the beautiful island of Manhattan was occupied by native peoples. In the 1600s, Dutch colonists from the Netherlands began taking over the island. They claimed Manhattan for the Dutch, dubbing the area New Netherland. They built a city called New Amsterdam. In 1658, the Dutch governor of New Netherland, Peter Stuyvesant, established the settlement of Nieuw (New) Haarlem. It was named after the city of Haarlem in his homeland.

But in 1664, the British took over the Dutch territory. They changed the names of the New Netherland territory and the city of New Amsterdam to New York, after the city of York in England. Nieuw Haarlem became known simply as Harlem. For more than 100 years, Harlem was mostly farmland and countryside. In the 1800s, people began building summer homes in the area as a place to get away from the hustle and bustle of New York City. Harlem became a neighborhood of prosperous white people living in solid brick houses and brownstone townhomes on wide tree-lined avenues.

BUILDING HARLEM

In the 1890s, real estate speculators began overbuilding in Harlem, hoping to attract white tenants and buyers who worked in the city. But in 1893, before they could find enough tenants or buyers, the United States experienced a stock market crash and an economic recession that lasted for years. This caused a housing market collapse, which turned out to be an advantage for African Americans looking for housing.

For years, it had been nearly impossible for African Americans to find decent housing in good New York neighborhoods. White landlords would only rent their worst properties in the most run-down areas to African Americans. Now, because of the housing collapse, white landowners were desperate to sell or rent their vacant buildings. They turned to African-American real estate agents, such as Philip A. Payton, John E. Nail, and Henry C. Parker, who purchased several rental properties themselves. These real estate agents also helped find African-American renters for white landlords.

In 1905, the first African Americans began moving into Harlem. However, landlords charged them significantly more per month than white renters. Unfortunately, it was common in New York to raise rents on African Americans. There were no laws to protect them against these unfair practices. However, many African Americans were willing to pay extra to have a decent place to live.

The Great Migration

In 1910, approximately 90 percent of all African Americans in the United States lived in the South. Of those, approximately 75 percent lived on farms. Then, beginning around 1916, came the great migration. Several million African Americans from the rural South moved to northern cities in hopes of making better lives for themselves.

Life had become more intolerable for African Americans in the

Father of Colored Harlem

Philip A. Payton opened his own real estate business in 1900. He struggled to make ends meet until 1905, when a white landlord asked Payton to manage an apartment building in Harlem where a murder had occurred. Payton filled the building with African-American tenants and went on to expand more African-American-owned businesses in Harlem, becoming a leader in the National Negro Business League. Although he lost some friends due to his domineering business style, Payton was a wealthy and influential man who helped open Harlem to African Americans. This earned him the title "Father of Colored Harlem."[1]

African-American sharecroppers were often very poor.

South after the end of the American Civil War
(1861–1865). Sharecropping was one of the few
ways of earning a living for many rural blacks.
However, it was an unfair system that kept blacks
in poverty. Sharecroppers could live on a plot of
land and farm it, but they had to give most of their
crop to the landowner, who was usually a rich white
man. The children of sharecroppers often began
working in the fields at age four or five in order to
help their families survive. Few were able to attend

school, so many sharecroppers were barely literate. Without basic literacy skills, it was even more difficult for sharecroppers to protect themselves from financial and legal exploitations. Then, the South was hit by drought and infestations of boll weevils. This caused several cotton crops to fail. With seasons of failed crops, sharecroppers spiraled into even deeper debts owed to landowners.

Racism in the South was another reason African Americans wanted to move north. The strict Jim Crow system of segregation in the South was degrading. It kept African Americans from exercising their right to vote and made it legal for whites to deny blacks equal access to basic rights and privileges. In addition, southern blacks lived with the ever-present fear of lynching, or murder by hanging. In contrast, the North offered job opportunities and communities where African Americans hoped to live safely, in peace.

Lynching in the South

In the South, a white person could abuse a black person for any reason—or none at all. Most African Americans would not fight back because fighting would put them and their loved ones at risk for being lynched. Lynchings were public murders carried out by racist mobs. Lynching victims were usually hanged by the neck from a tree or a building, and sometimes they were mutilated or burned. Whites used lynching as a way to intimidate blacks so they would not try to better their situations. Some people were lynched for voting, demanding respect, or suing a white man.

Another important aspect of the great migration was World War I (1914–1918). Once Congress declared war on Germany in the spring of 1917, the United States needed to supply its armies. It needed people to build ships and equip thousands of soldiers with uniforms, food, supplies, weapons, and ammunition. Tens of thousands of jobs opened up in various factories in the North. African Americans poured into cities with those factories hoping to find work as part of the war effort.

Jim Crow

Jim Crow was a system of racism and oppression against black people that operated as early as the first half of the nineteenth century until the mid-1960s. The term *Jim Crow* comes from the minstrel show song "Jump, Jim Crow." A white entertainer wearing charcoal makeup sang and danced in a ridiculous imitation of a black man when performing the song. Minstrel shows were very popular beginning in the 1820s with white audiences throughout the United States and Europe. The shows, however, were extremely demeaning to African Americans because they perpetuated the notion of black inferiority.

Jim Crow laws and attitudes were based on the false belief that white people were superior to people of color in every way. White supremacists created the Jim Crow system to dominate African Americans and make them afraid to strive for equality. Beginning in 1896, one of the main tools of Jim Crow was enforced segregation of public services. In the South, black people were banned from public facilities meant for white people, including schools, hospitals, buses, trains, libraries, restaurants, public parks, restrooms, and water fountains. The unspoken rules of Jim Crow etiquette were probably even more oppressive and humiliating because they required blacks to treat whites with deference at all times.

Chicago, Detroit, and Cleveland saw huge growths in African-American populations during World War I— so did New York.

When New York's midtown area began redeveloping, whites pushed African Americans out. They relocated to Harlem. Some former midtowners who moved to Harlem were intellectuals and artists who would become pivotal figures in the Harlem Renaissance.

WHITE FLIGHT

Many white residents of Harlem were furious about the neighborhood becoming integrated. White homeowners and businessmen tried to find ways to keep African Americans out. Some claimed that their property values and way of life would be destroyed if black people moved in. Organizations such as the Hudson Realty Company and the Property Owners Protective Agency were created for the purpose of buying Harlem properties where African Americans lived and evicting them—and securing large areas for whites only.

But African Americans were also engaging in the real estate fight for Harlem turf. They were buying and leasing properties and renting them to other

Safe for Democracy

In 1917, the United States declared war against Germany. President Woodrow Wilson said war was necessary to make the world safe for democracy. Many African Americans recognized the United States' hypocrisy in proclaiming democracy while denying citizens of color their basic civil rights, but they could not agree on how to respond. Some said black men should stay home—they should not risk their lives for a country that oppressed them. Others said that going to war for their country would prove their loyalty to the United States, and that a grateful nation would grant them civil rights after the war.

blacks. One important battle was over the Watt Estate. The Watt Estate was a mansion with extensive gardens that encompassed an entire city block. In 1913, white politicians wanted Harlem to purchase the property to build a playground for white children. Despite their vigorous campaign to secure this vital section of Harlem for whites, the politicians failed. In 1914, the mansion was transformed into the Libya Hotel— Harlem's first African-American nightclub.

When the white residents realized they could not stop the influx of African Americans to Harlem, they began moving away. This made room for more black people to move in. Not only African Americans, but also immigrants from Africa and the West Indies brought even more cultural diversity to Harlem. Before 1905, Harlem was a mostly white community. By 1930, more than 200,000 people of African heritage were calling Harlem home.

A man speaks with a teller at Dunbar National Bank.
Dunbar was a bank in Harlem for blacks.

Young girls in Harlem dancing the Charleston

Black Mecca

arlem was a kaleidoscope of colors and cultures. People made up nicknames for each other and the different types of people who lived there. The educated northerners were called dicties because their dictation, or speech, was grammatically correct. Southern blacks who had rushed north to escape lynching were called Russians. The slang term for West Indian immigrants was monkey chasers. People who acted submissive to whites were dubbed handkerchief-heads.

The cultural and class differences between the people living in Harlem were many. But one thing united them: they were all of African descent. This meant they all were discriminated against by the dominant white society. This one common factor created a united goal—to uplift the race.

BLACK ORGANIZATIONS

To make life better for all African Americans, educated leaders in Harlem, Chicago, and black colleges throughout the United States began establishing organizations dedicated to uniting and strengthening their people. Foremost among these

Harlem Slang

The people of Harlem developed their own ways of talking and slang to describe their lives. Some examples include,
"Air out: leave
Beating up your gums: talking to no purpose
Cold: exceeding, well, etc.
Cut: doing something well
Diddy-Wah-Diddy: a far place
Dig: understand
Dumb to the fact: you don't know what you are talking about
Gif up off of me: quit talking about me
Hauling: fleeing on foot"[1]

organizations were the National Association for the
Advancement of Colored People (NAACP), founded
in 1909, and the National Urban League, founded
in 1910. Both organizations established headquarters
in Harlem. The first ten years of their work for racial
progress helped usher in the Harlem Renaissance.

The NAACP grew out of a fellowship of African-
American leaders called the Niagara Movement.
The Niagara Movement was dedicated to promoting
civil rights and ending racism, segregation, and
oppression of African Americans. But few whites
paid attention to the Niagara Movement—that
is, until a white humanitarian and reformer
named Mary White Ovington wrote about it. She
believed racism could only be fought by interracial
partnerships in which white and black people work
together. Some black leaders did not trust white
people's intentions. They wanted to exclude whites
from the movement. But other African-American
leaders, such as writer W. E. B. DuBois, believed
Ovington was right—the United States was too
steeped in racism to accept African Americans on
their own merits. They needed the help of white
people who believed in their cause.

In 1909, the several African-American leaders, including DuBois, met with several white leaders of social reform and established the NAACP. Its purpose was to oppose racism in all its forms. This included segregation and discrimination in housing, education, jobs, voting, and transportation, and to fight for constitutional rights for African Americans. The NAACP was interracial, allowing blacks and whites to work together toward these goals. Knowing communication was crucial to the growth of the movement, the NAACP appointed DuBois as the editor of its monthly magazine, the *Crisis.* Under DuBois's leadership the magazine would become the primary forum for African Americans to learn, discuss, and spread ideas. It would become a pivotal part of the Harlem Renaissance.

Like the NAACP, the National Urban League was an interracial organization dedicated to helping make life better for African Americans. It was founded by

Race Riots

In the early twentieth century, several riots caused by racism erupted in various areas of the United States. During these riots, mobs of white people attacked black neighborhoods, lynching and beating people and torching their homes, schools, and businesses. Many of these riots happened because white people wanted to punish African Americans who dared to stand up for themselves in the face of racism. Others occurred when employers hired black workers to replace white union workers who were on strike. Additionally, many whites falsely accused blacks of crimes in order to spark more violence.

George Edmund Haynes

George Edmund Haynes was born in 1880 in Pine Bluff, Arkansas, to poor but hardworking parents. After graduating from Fisk University in 1903, he earned a master's degree in social work from Yale. He then graduated from New York School of Philanthropy in 1910. Two years later, Haynes earned a PhD in economics from Columbia University. Haynes's doctoral dissertation, *The Negro at Work in New York City*, was published in 1912. It called attention to the economic plight of urban African Americans. Haynes was instrumental in developing training programs for African-American social workers. After helping to establish the National Urban League, he served as its executive director from 1911 to 1918.

George Edmund Haynes, the first African American to earn a PhD from Columbia University, and Ruth Standish Baldwin, a white New York City philanthropist. The Urban League's first efforts focused on helping migrants from the rural South find housing and adjust to life in New York. It hoped to protect them from being exploited by white northerners.

During the great migration, many southern blacks had no means of financing their journeys north. Several employment agencies took advantage of this. They found white sponsors who would pay travel expenses for southern blacks in exchange for several years of unpaid domestic labor. Many African Americans who signed such contracts for labor became caught in another type of slavery. If they tried to leave their sponsors, they could lose all their possessions.

It was this unscrupulous activity that the Urban League first began fighting, but its efforts soon expanded. The Urban League took on many social problems, working to improve housing, employment, sanitation, health services, and even playgrounds in New York. To further their goals, the Urban League trained social workers to deal with the variety of problems that arose as so many people converged on Harlem.

The Urban League also published a magazine. *Opportunity* printed creative writing by African Americans as well as news and information about issues of race and society. Like the NAACP's the *Crisis* magazine, *Opportunity* would become an important part of the Harlem Renaissance.

Social Life

Due to the work of these and other organizations, Harlem quickly gained the reputation of being a safe haven for African Americans. It became known as the black mecca—the best place to be. It was a beacon of pride for African Americans throughout the United States. Harlem also attracted artists, musicians, writers, and many African-American professionals such as doctors, lawyers, and educators.

Churches also played a major role in strengthening the Harlem neighborhood. Harlem churches were more than places of worship—they offered a uniquely African-American perspective on life. The pastors of such churches preached on religion, taught about social and racial justice, encouraged education, provided programs for orphans and the elderly, and helped find jobs and housing for the poor. Churches got involved in many civil rights activities.

On Sunday mornings, rich and poor alike dressed in their Sunday finest and often spent all day at church. There, even the newest immigrants to Harlem could find immediate acceptance. The music in Harlem churches was lively, incorporating spiritual songs from the South as well as European and African-inspired styles. People often ate meals together after the morning services, followed by joining in on one of many afternoon parades down Harlem streets.

Parades and Strolling

Parades were very popular in Harlem and happened for many reasons. They might have been to celebrate the founding of a new organization or business, honor the funeral of a prominent citizen, or observe a holiday. Most parades featured lively marching bands dressed in colorful, fancy uniforms. Honorees rode along in automobiles. It was not the custom in Harlem to merely watch a parade pass by. Most folks who were able usually joined in and marched along in step to the brilliant music. When it was warm enough, no Sunday afternoon went by without at least one parade.

Strolling was another uniquely Harlem, but unstructured,

The Silent Protest Parade

The first major peaceful protest by African Americans happened on July 28, 1917, in New York City. It was sponsored by the NAACP in response to the latest riot in East Saint Louis, Illinois, where many were murdered by white mobs. At the head of the parade marched 300 children and 5,000 women dressed in white, followed by thousands of men, many of whom had fought in World War I. No one spoke a word, but African-American Boy Scouts handed out leaflets titled *Why Do We March?* to observers. The leaflets read,

We march because by the Grace of God and the force of truth, the dangerous, hampering walls of prejudice and inhuman injustices must fall.

We march because we want to make impossible a repetition of Waco, Memphis and East St. Louis by arousing the conscience of the country, and to bring the murderers of our brothers, sisters, and innocent children to justice.

We march because we deem it a crime to be silent in the face of such barbaric acts.

We march because we are thoroughly opposed to Jim-Crow Cars, Segregation, Discrimination, Disenfranchisement, LYNCHING and the host of evils that are forced on us.[2]

social activity. Strolling in Harlem did not mean merely walking down the street. It meant walking along certain streets for the purpose of connecting with others. If people felt like socializing, on any day of the week, they would dress in their best clothes and go out for a stroll hoping to meet others doing the same. They would stop to chat and joke with friends and make new acquaintances. Young people out strolling often hoped to meet someone they might like to date. Harlem author James Weldon Johnson explained that strolling in Harlem was "not simply going out for a walk; it [was] more like going out for an adventure."[3]

Harlem had indeed become a mecca for African Americans. This atmosphere of racial unity helped set the stage for the flowering of African-American culture that came to be known as the Harlem Renaissance.

W. E. B. DuBois would become a major voice of the Harlem Renaissance.

Booker T. Washington represented the old approach to reaching equality for African Americans.

THE NEW NEGRO MOVEMENT

fter the abolition of slavery in 1865, many African-American intellectuals began writing about how African Americans could forge a new identity for themselves—an identity of pride, prosperity, and equality. In the late 1800s,

the idea of a new African-American identity became
the subject of many essays, sermons, and poems.
This eventually led to the growth of the New Negro
movement in the early 1900s. The movement was the
mother of the Harlem Renaissance. Its undisputed
father was DuBois.

W. E. B. DuBois and Booker T. Washington

DuBois was the first African American to earn
a PhD from Harvard. His book *The Souls of Black Folk*
was published in 1903. The book describes the
evils of racism and what it did to black people who
experienced it. It also celebrates the strength of
African Americans and calls for them to stand up to
racial injustice. With this book, DuBois contradicted
the man who had been the foremost African-
American leader, Booker T. Washington.

Washington, a former slave, was very practical
in his approach to black education. In the South,
many African Americans were barely surviving.
He preached that African Americans should strive
to learn practical skills and trades and work hard.
By so doing, Washington felt blacks would prove
themselves to whites as being worthy of equality.
Washington did not believe African Americans

Booker T. Washington

Booker T. Washington was a slave until he was about ten years old, when President Abraham Lincoln signed the Emancipation Proclamation in 1863. Washington worked his way up from poverty, earned his education, and founded the Tuskegee Institute, an agricultural school for African Americans. Washington gained a good deal of financial support for his school from white benefactors, largely due to his message that blacks should accommodate whites' dominant role in society without fighting it. Although he secretly supported the NAACP's fight for civil rights, he would not publicly say so, fearing it would undermine his position with both white and black supporters.

should fight openly for their civil rights. He feared this would inflame white anger and retaliation against blacks. He argued that eventually white people would recognize the virtue of hardworking blacks and someday share the blessings of liberty with them. He encouraged blacks to be patient and quiet in the meantime.

DuBois accused Washington of discouraging African Americans from pursuing a higher education. In fact, this was untrue. Washington encouraged college attendance for anyone who was able. But he believed not everyone was suited to intellectual pursuits, so he advocated technical training.

DuBois's stand against Washington's ideals resonated with many people, but it also caused division. Those who revered the conservative Washington wanted to believe his way was the right and safe way to earn equality. But it had only seemed to encourage southern whites to further oppress their black neighbors. During the era of Washingtonian pacifism, segregation laws abounded and lynching increased. The more radical DuBois argued that it was time for African Americans to stand up for themselves.

THE TALENTED TENTH

One of DuBois's favorite ideas was his notion of the Talented Tenth. DuBois defined the Talented Tenth as the 10 percent of African Americans who were educated and successful. He believed gifted blacks who achieved social status in the white culture would prove to whites they were wrong about blacks being inferior. DuBois believed outperforming whites in various educational and social settings would lead to integration and equality with whites. According to DuBois, it was the obligation of the Talented Tenth to be the leaders of African-American culture. They had to set an example for the rest of the race. He believed these ideals would eventually work their way down to the lower classes through the efforts of the elite tenth. These ideas quickly caught on with many educated middle-class African Americans.

"One ever feels his two-ness,—an American, a Negro; two souls, two thoughts . . . two warring ideals in one dark body. . . . The history of the American Negro is the history of this strife. . . . He would not Africanize America, for America has too much to teach the world and Africa. He would not bleach his Negro soul in a flood of white Americanism, for he knows that Negro blood has a message for the world. He simply wishes to make it possible . . . to be both a Negro and an American, without being cursed and spit upon . . . without having the doors of Opportunity closed roughly in his face."[1]
   —W. E. B. DuBois, The Souls of Black Folk

While DuBois wanted African Americans to focus on gaining a classical European-style education— so they could compete on equal intellectual ground with the best-educated whites—James Weldon Johnson and Alain Locke brought a slightly different view to the New Negro movement. Johnson's 1912 novel, *The Autobiography of an Ex-Colored Man*, inspired many creative people during the Harlem Renaissance to explore ideas of race and what it meant to be black in a white society. This would become a common theme among Harlem Renaissance writers. Johnson was also one of the first mentors of young black writers, musicians, and artists to encourage them to look to their cultural roots for inspiration. This included folk tales, spirituals (the music created by US slaves), and blues and ragtime music. To make their African-American heritage more available to younger artists, Johnson researched and compiled two important anthologies, *The Book of American Negro Poetry* in 1922 and *The Book of American Negro Spirituals* in 1925.

Locke, a professor of philosophy at Howard University, also advocated that blacks should explore their African heritage. He also thought it was crucial for them to study classical Greek and German to broaden their minds and reach a wider audience. Like DuBois, Locke's mission was to change the way the world viewed black people and to earn respect for their race. He believed racial equality would come through no other means. Locke's voice was very influential in the New Negro movement and the Harlem Renaissance. He created a literary magazine, the *Stylus*, and encouraged students to publish their work. "We have enough talent now to begin to have a movement—and to express a school of thought," Locke wrote to one of his students.[2]

The Untalented Ninetieth

So far, the New Negro movement seemed to focus on uplifting the entire race by cultivating those with leadership potential. But this left about 90 percent of blacks out of the picture. The average black citizen did not want to wait for the Talented Tenth to make the world a better place in the future. They wanted a better life now. While DuBois, Locke, and other leaders were busy encouraging the Talented Tenth, another leader arose to inspire the rest of the African-American population: Marcus Garvey.

Garvey, a Jamaican, founded the Universal Negro Improvement Association (UNIA) in 1914 in his home country. Inspired by Washington's autobiography, *Up from Slavery*, and the success of the Tuskegee Institute, Garvey traveled to the United States. He wanted to learn how he could start a school in Jamaica similar to the Tuskegee Institute. His experience with colonialism in the West Indies and racism in the West had convinced him whites would never integrate equally with blacks. He believed people of African heritage could only achieve freedom by reclaiming Africa. His goal was to unite millions of blacks from all over the world, return to Africa, and free their home continent of white authority forever.

In 1916, Garvey brought his ideas and the UNIA to Harlem. There, he began reaching out to those he affectionately called "the untalented ninetieth"— the poor and working class African Americans.[3] An experienced printer and gifted writer, he started a

Marcus Garvey, right

magazine called the *Negro World*, which became hugely popular. His ideas about black pride, unity, and reclaiming Africa for Africans also caught attention.

Tens of thousands of people became members of the UNIA. People who held positions of leadership wore fancy military-like uniforms. Garvey's UNIA parades down Harlem streets were flashy and full of black pride. Garvey represented a new kind of New Negro—the kind who did not have to be highly educated, rich, or successful to be proud.

Harlem's First Heroes

Meanwhile, cultural identity and a sense of community grew in Harlem. After World War I ended in 1918, the victorious US soldiers began coming home. Among them was the 369th Infantry, also known as the Harlem Hellfighters, an all-black unit of soldiers. On February 17, 1919, the Hellfighters' ship docked in New York Harbor and the veterans marched out and headed home to Harlem, led by an all-black marching band of 60 men. The governor of New York and the entire city came out to welcome the Hellfighters as heroes, but their reception in Harlem was even better.

Thousands lined the streets, crowded onto balconies and rooftops, and leaned out of windows to welcome their heroes home. At first, the soldiers marched in military precision, but when they got on their home turf, the musicians broke into the song "Here Comes My Daddy." The soldiers danced in step down their beloved Harlem streets. The crowds went wild. Mothers, wives, and girlfriends broke through the ranks to reach their men, hugging and kissing them and crying for joy.

These veterans added a new facet to the New Negro movement. The Hellfighters were fighting men, trained to stand up for themselves and their nation. Their experiences of racial integration in Europe brought new perspectives to Harlem. The

The Harlem Hellfighters

The 369th Infantry was the first all-black unit to fight in World War I. The US military would not allow black and white soldiers to serve together in combat, so the 369th was assigned to the French army. The French soldiers treated the men of the 369th as equals, fighting side-by-side and forming friendships, despite the US military's demands that the French not fraternize with black soldiers.

The 369th Infantry earned its nickname as the Harlem Hellfighters for its strength and tenacity in battle. The men served 191 days of duty, longer than any other unit—and not one man was captured and they lost no ground to the enemy. Sadly, almost one-third of the Hellfighters died in combat. They were the first African Americans to earn medals on a foreign field of battle. The French government awarded the 369th 171 of its highest honor medals: the Croix de Guerre, or "cross of war," to recognize the group's acts of bravery in the face of the enemy.

Many people hoped the soldiers' sacrifices would lead to equal rights and better treatment for all African Americans after the war. But the United States still refused democracy to the very men who had fought so hard to protect it.

James Reese Europe

James Reese Europe was a musical pioneer who helped popularize African-American musical groups. He also led the 369th Infantry's marching band. Europe's band toured France in 1918 and is credited for introducing France to US jazz music. In 1919, after leading the Hellfighters' triumphant march home to Harlem, he launched a tour of the nation and was hailed everywhere for his "gorgeous racket of syncopation and jazzing."[4] Europe was also respected for his keen mind and professionalism. He mentored many black musicians and helped them get work throughout the United States and Europe.

Hellfighters may have been Harlem's first heroes, but they were not the last. These brave men strode into Harlem on the cusp of the Harlem Renaissance, an era that would usher in a new kind of African-American hero fighting another kind of battle—the battle for equality and cultural identity.

The Harlem Hellfighters became a symbol of black pride.

James Weldon Johnson

INTRODUCING THE WRITERS

N o one can pinpoint the exact beginning of the Harlem Renaissance, but 1920 seems to be the year it branched off from the New Negro movement to take on a life of its own. That was when several young African-American writers, inspired by the teachings and writings of DuBois, Johnson, Locke, and others, began publishing their work in African-American publications. These included magazines, newspapers, and literary journals such as the *Crisis*, *Negro World*, *Opportunity*, and Locke's the *Stylus*. Publications such as these were widely read by African Americans, but the New Negro writers wanted a wider audience.

New Negro Publications

In the 1920s, the publishing industry, like the rest of society, was dominated by white culture. Whites largely ignored African Americans' contributions to the collective culture. The biggest publications employed white writers and editors who catered to their white audiences. Any images or stories of African Americans were nearly always negative or employed racial stereotypes that made black people seem inferior. To combat the demoralizing influence of white perceptions of Negro culture, African Americans created their own publications.

African-American publications were crucial to the development of black culture and the New Negro ideal. They provided a forum for news, information, education, and creative expression for a people who were oppressed and marginalized by the dominant culture. They strengthened African-American identity and pride in many ways. However, they did not help dispel the dominant culture's negative view of minorities because few whites ever read them. As long as segregation kept the races from interacting, whites would remain ignorant of African Americans. This ignorance would allow whites to continue ignoring and marginalizing blacks.

The Harlem Renaissance leaders believed a first crucial step toward undoing segregation and racism would be for African-American writers to gain a white audience. Reading the works of African-American writers could show whites that African Americans were equal human beings. Once whites realized this, society would have to change. It would have to accept African Americans as true citizens and dismantle segregation.

The Civic Club Dinner

On March 21, 1924, Harlem's literary leaders hosted an interracial event that would be pivotal in bringing the Harlem Renaissance to the world. Charles S. Johnson, the editor of *Opportunity*, organized the event. He invited prestigious white editors and publishers, African-American writers, and influential leaders of organizations such as the NAACP, the YMCA, and the Urban League. Johnson saw this event as a type of coming out party—a way to celebrate and bring more attention to African-American creativity. He hoped the white publishing establishment would begin making room for New Negro writers in their publications. Locke, the evening's master of ceremonies, told his distinguished audience these young writers possessed "a spiritual wealth" that could provide a new vision of the black race in the United States.[1]

The outcome of this dinner was that white publishers, who had long ignored black writers, now became interested in them. They realized they could profit from the growing New Negro movement and on white readers' new interest in black culture. The editor of *Harper's* magazine asked to publish Countee Cullen's poems

Countee Cullen

Countee Cullen was an exceptional student who distinguished himself early in life while attending the nearly all-white DeWitt Clinton High School in Manhattan. He began winning poetry competitions in 1921 and publishing poetry in various magazines and journals. Cullen published his first volume of poetry, *Color*, in 1925, when he was a senior at New York University. Locke praised Cullen's work "for portraying the experience of African Americans in the vocabulary and poetic forms of the classical tradition but with a personal intimacy."[2] DuBois also praised Cullen and looked to this young poet to raise the image of the black race.

Countee Cullen was one of the black writers who benefited from the Civic Club dinner.

in November 1924. *Survey Graphic*, a monthly magazine devoted to social work and humanitarian concerns, asked Locke to compile a special issue devoted entirely to African-American life and the question of race relations.

Harlem in *Survey Graphic*

Locke saw *Survey Graphic* as his chance to launch the image of the New Negro and establish "Harlem as the world's race capital."[3] He avoided any themes that would show African Americans as a societal problem.

Instead, he focused on works that uplifted the race. He solicited essays by several prominent New Negro leaders, including DuBois, Charles Johnson, and James Weldon Johnson, and he wrote two essays himself. Also featured was poetry by Cullen, Angelina Grimke, Langston Hughes, Claude McKay, Jean Toomer, and Anne Spencer.

This special issue of *Survey Graphic*, titled "Harlem: Mecca of the New Negro," came out in March 1925. It was hugely popular among its progressive white readership and with African-American readers. In fact, *Survey Graphic* sold approximately twice as many copies of this issue than any other in the history of the magazine. It was so successful that Locke began working on an expanded version to be published later that year as a book called *The New Negro: Voices of the Harlem Renaissance*. In just one issue, the *Survey Graphic* had brought the Harlem Renaissance to the notice of tens of thousands of readers, both black and white.

INSPIRATION

Creative people are inspired by many things including the beauty of nature and witnessing important events. But they are also inspired by each other's work. This is what happened during the

Harlem Renaissance—readers, viewers, and listeners became inspired, and even more new artists were born.

Jean Toomer

Jean Toomer was of mixed heritage. In his search for identity, he wandered the country "working as a bodybuilder, a welder, a student of agriculture, a Ford salesman, a physical-education teacher, a hobo."[4] In Georgia, Toomer discovered his African-American roots. Inspired by blues and folk tales, Toomer wrote *Cane*, a small volume of poems and short stories, in 1923. Black leaders asked Toomer to make more "race contributions."[5] But Toomer did not consider himself an African American. He had written *Cane* to memorialize southern blacks' way of life before it was changed forever. Toomer never published another book.

One such artist was Aaron Douglas. Deeply inspired by *Survey Graphic*'s special issue, he quit his job teaching high school in Missouri. He moved to Harlem to devote his life to his art. This move made an enormous impact on the Harlem Renaissance.

Soon after Douglas arrived in Harlem, he found multiple jobs as an artist. DuBois hired him as an illustrator for the *Crisis* magazine. James Weldon Johnson hired him to produce art for *Opportunity*. Locke hired him to work on several paintings and design the cover of *The New Negro: Voices of the Harlem Renaissance*.

There had been some controversy around some of the images featured in the *Survey Graphic* special issue. The issue's cover and much of the artwork had been contributed by a white European artist named Winold

Reiss. Reiss was well known and respected for his portrayals of various racial types. But many African Americans wanted to see more work by black artists. Douglas came to Harlem at the most opportune time. The Harlem Renaissance leaders saw Douglas's art as the perfect blend of African folk art roots, classical European training, and modern techniques. It embodied and expressed the true spirit of the Harlem Renaissance.

When *The New Negro* was published in the fall of 1925, DuBois called it "the best Negro book in the past ten years."[6] And it

Langston Hughes

Writer Langston Hughes managed to thrive despite racism. Soon after graduating from high school, Hughes wrote the poem "The Negro Speaks of Rivers" and sent it to Jessie Fauset, editor of the *Crisis*. Fauset, immediately impressed with the poem's beauty and dignity, published it in the *Crisis* in 1921.

Hughes moved to New York to study at Columbia University, but he was more interested in Harlem life and culture. He struck up a close friendship with Cullen, who introduced him to other Harlem writers and editors. In 1922, Hughes took a job as a busboy on a ship. This gave him the chance to see the world and provided him the solitude he needed to write. He sent the poems he wrote while on the ship to Cullen, who recited them at literary gatherings. Many of Hughes's poems became hugely popular.

Hughes traveled to Africa, where he was both enchanted by the land and people and horrified by the racism of the Europeans who had colonized there. He returned to Harlem in 1924 much wiser than when he had left—and he was welcomed back as an important Harlem Renaissance writer.

Claude McKay

Claude McKay was born in Jamaica. His famous poem "If We Must Die" protests racism and lynching. In 1922, he published *Harlem Shadows*, a volume of poetry. McKay's 1928 novel, *Home to Harlem*, became the first best-selling novel by an African-American author, but its honest depiction of Harlem's negative aspects stirred controversy. DuBois did not appreciate McKay's explicit work and said reading *Home to Harlem* made him feel like he needed to take a bath. But James Weldon Johnson said, "Claude McKay's poetry was one of the great forces in bringing about what is often called the 'Negro Literary Renaissance'"[7]

was to be one of the most important books to come out of the Harlem Renaissance. It includes most of the content from the *Survey Graphic* special issue and features additional fiction, poetry, and art from even more African-American writers and artists. *The New Negro* heightened awareness about the renaissance that was happening in Harlem and around the nation. As they created the New Negro identity, African Americans' voices and images would continue to inspire even more creativity.

Langston Hughes became one of the most popular poets
of the Harlem Renaissance.

Waiters at Small's Paradise

Diversity
and Disagreement

y the 1920s, the Harlem Renaissance
was gaining a good deal of notice from
outsiders. White New Yorkers came to Harlem
for the music and liquor. They also came to meet
the rising stars of the neighborhood. Some young

writers, artists, and musicians began to enjoy a measure of fame and attention, especially from rich white folks at parties and clubs who were excited by what they considered the primitive aspects of black culture. But this kind of attention was not what Harlem's leaders had in mind.

CONTROLLING THE BLACK IMAGE

Older leaders such as DuBois and Locke wanted to control the black image, supporting only the work they considered beautiful and uplifting to the race. DuBois especially disapproved of anything that might make African Americans look bad in the eyes of the world. Whites already considered blacks inferior, immoral, and primitive. DuBois wanted his people to prove them wrong. He felt very strongly that all writing, art, and music created by African Americans should be racial propaganda—that is, work that portrayed African

Fire!!

In 1926, several of the younger and more radical Harlem creatives compiled an experimental literary magazine they called *Fire!!* Featuring art by Aaron Douglas and writings by Hurston, Cullen, Hughes, Wallace Thurmon, and Bruce Nugent, *Fire!!* ignited the anger of Harlem leaders such as DuBois who called it decadent and low. The magazine included poems in free-form verse and discussions of blues and jazz. DuBois considered these art forms less prestigious than others. Only one issue of *Fire!!* was printed and, ironically, the unsold copies were destroyed in a fire.

Americans in the best possible light. Only when whites accepted blacks as equals would integration become a reality.

This led to some sharp disagreements among Harlem's creative circles. Many of the younger Harlem writers wanted more freedom of expression. They argued that they should be free to portray all aspects of African-American life and culture— the beautiful as well as the ugly. Hughes, McKay, and Zora Neale Hurston especially disliked the idea of racial propaganda. Their stories, poems, and plays included characters that used slang and street language— even some who were prostitutes, vagabonds, and criminals. This disgusted DuBois and his Talented Tenth. They thought the younger artists were being vulgar and bringing down the image of the race.

Cullen was one of the few young writers who agreed that black writers

*Hurston did not like DuBois's idea
of making art that was racial propaganda.*

should keep some aspects of African-American
culture to themselves. Unlike many of his peers,
Cullen wrote mainly in European style, avoiding black
vernacular. But while he agreed with DuBois on

some points, he also disagreed about the idea of art as propaganda. He once wrote,

> If I am going to be a poet at all, then I am going to be POET and not NEGRO POET . . . I shall not write of negro subjects for the purpose of propaganda. That is not what a poet is concerned with. Of course, when the emotion rising out of the fact that I am a Negro is strong, I express it. But that is another matter.[2]

Cullen also scorned some of Hughes's work as placing "too much emphasis on strictly Negro themes."[3] In their turn, Hughes and other writers took offense at Cullen's words, saying he would rather be white than black.

PRIMITIVISM

The idea of primitivism was all the rage in the 1920s, especially among white intellectuals. After World War I, many whites began to feel Western

Hurston's Lingo

Hurston had a way with words—and a way of inventing new words. When she moved to Harlem, she took up residence in a boardinghouse with other writers and artists where they all lived a delightfully bohemian life, painting the walls in reds and blacks and partying a good deal. Hurston dubbed the house Niggerati Manor, and the name stuck.

Hurston also came up with a new term for the wealthy white patrons who gave financial assistance to the black artist community. She called these humanitarians toward black people Negrotarians. That name also stuck.

European-style culture had lost its way in the modern age. The ravages of war and unrestrained industrialism were killing not only bodies but human souls. Some white people began to idealize the people and cultures they considered to be primitive, such as Native Americans and blacks. According to this philosophy, so-called primitive people were closer to the Earth and to their own natures—they had a kind of purity whites had lost. Primitives were thought to be more open, sensual, free, and spiritual.

Many whites believed primitive ways of being could lead them into a simpler, happier life. This was a significant reason why any art, music, or literature that displayed primitivism was so popular in mainstream society. It was also one of the reasons why whites came to Harlem. Many rich white people wanted to surround themselves with anything considered primitive, as if

Sterling Brown

Sterling Brown was a poet, writer, and English professor. While teaching in Virginia, he became fascinated by the folk tales and lives of rural African Americans, which he found more inspiring than what he had learned in colleges in the North. Brown began writing black vernacular poems and stories, which were published in *Opportunity* and in anthologies by Cullen and James Weldon Johnson. He identified five themes central to the Harlem Renaissance: "1) Africa as a source of race pride, 2) black American heroes, 3) racial political propaganda, 4) the black folk tradition, and 5) candid self-revelation."[4]

buying black art and books, listening to black music, and partying with black people might set them free.

Some Harlem Renaissance writers and artists felt this embracing of the primitive aspects of humanity allowed them more freedom to express themselves. They could throw off the traditional ways of behaving and tap into their wild sides. But others thought primitivism was just another way to stereotype African Americans as inferior and would hurt racial progress by keeping the races separate.

THE GODMOTHER

Charlotte Louise Van Der Veer Quick Mason was one white woman whose belief in primitivism had a major impact on the Harlem Renaissance. Mason became interested in the New Negro ideal in 1927 when she heard a lecture by Locke on African art. Locke quickly befriended the rich elderly lady. He brought several talented young African-American writers and artists to meet Mason. Mason promised to give money to those whose work embodied her primitive idealism.

Mason's financial support to Locke, Hughes, Hurston, and others helped them pursue their work. She told them to refer to her as Godmother, partly because she wanted to avoid publicity, and partly because that was the role she wanted to play in their lives. She even had her godchildren, the African-American artists she supported, sit on a low stool at her feet while she talked with them.

In addition to supplying her protégés with money, fancy clothes, tickets to operas, cars, and good food, she asked that they account to her for what they did with their time. Mason also wanted control over their work. She insisted that Hughes spend all his talent on writing poems

Carl Van Vechten

Carl Van Vechten was a rich white patron of the arts who also had an important influence on the Harlem Renaissance. Van Vechten had always been attracted to African-American culture and music, even as a boy. As an adult, he became a successful photographer and critic of art, music, literature, and culture. Van Vechten began spending time in Harlem interviewing writers and artists and listening to blues and jazz, and he brought many famous white people with him who also learned to love Harlem's nightlife. Van Vechten's articles about Harlem—where to go and what to see—helped make Harlem the most popular nightspot for white New Yorkers in the 1920s.

Van Vechten also helped many African-American writers, such as Hughes, become published and also wrote favorable critiques of their work, which helped gain them a wider white readership. However, some African Americans did not trust Van Vechten's motives, thinking he was only interested in profiting from black culture. When Van Vechten published a novel titled *Nigger Heaven*—the common name for the theater balconies where blacks had to sit so they would not be near whites—many African Americans were deeply offended and felt they had been exploited.

she felt would save the black race. Mason also financed Hurston's travels to collect African-American folklore, but on the condition that Mason would own all Hurston's research. Hurston was not allowed to publish anything without Mason's permission.

Mason exerted a powerful influence on the most promising and prolific writers and artists of the Harlem Renaissance. This had positive and negative effects. The financial help she gave enabled them to focus on their creative work, but the money she gave kept them dependent on her and under her control. Eventually, all of Mason's godchildren broke away from her to pursue their work without her interference. ⌐

Locke received some support from Mason.

*Many people still enjoy the art of Archibald Motley
and other Harlem Renaissance artists.*

THE ARTS
AND THE ARTISTS

The Harlem Renaissance began with literature,
but it also encompassed many other facets
of the creative arts. During this period, African
Americans found new forms of expression through
the visual arts—painting, drawing, sculpture, and

photography—and others through the performing arts—theatre, film, singing, and dancing.

Historically, the United States was no place for black visual artists. Despite the art world's reputation for being open-minded, the art establishment remained bigoted, especially toward African Americans. Artistically inclined blacks in the United States might be able to do conventional types of art, such as painting landscapes. Still, white prejudice made studying art seriously or experimenting with new styles nearly impossible for them. And many art galleries and museums not only refused to display the work of black artists, they also did not welcome black visitors. If black artists wanted to pursue art seriously, most of them went to Europe. Paris, France, was especially welcoming to black artists and their work.

Art and Oppression

African Americans did not have a rich art history of their own to draw

Augusta Savage Protests

Augusta Savage was the first African-American artist to publicly oppose racism in the white art world. She was denied a place in a summer art school for women because two Alabama artists did not want "a colored girl" traveling with them to Paris.[1] Although Savage's protests were published in both white and African-American newspapers, she was barred by the French government from attending. This earned her a good reputation as a civil rights activist and a bad reputation in the art world. Her fellow African-American artists thought her confrontational style may have contributed to her being excluded from other exhibitions and galleries.

from or build upon. Slavery, poverty, segregation, and racism had kept blacks out of the art world for years. Only a few could make it to Europe to study and show their work. As a result, the art world in the United States suffered from a lack of African-American presence in the visual arts. The few African Americans who were able to pursue their art tended to devote their energies to proving themselves adept in classical art styles. This is why most art by African Americans before the Harlem Renaissance was imitative.

Many African Americans also shied away from portraying images of black people and culture because of all the negative images that already existed of African Americans. Minstrels in charcoal makeup called blackface and cartoons portraying racist, stereotyped depictions of African Americans were everywhere. Many whites found such images amusing and harmless, but they were demeaning to blacks and damaging to race relations.

DuBois acknowledged this fear of black images, but he encouraged

Black Is Beautiful

Douglas was passionate about helping other African Americans recognize the beauty in blackness. In a letter to his fiancée, Alta Sawyer, Douglas wrote, "We are possessed, you know, with the idea that it is necessary to be white, to be beautiful. Nine times out of ten it is just the reverse. It takes lots of training or a tremendous effort to down the idea that thin lips and a straight nose is the apogee of beauty. But once free you can look back with a sigh of relief and wonder how anyone could be so deluded."[2]

African Americans to get past it and begin painting, drawing, and sculpting likenesses of the New Negro. DuBois knew white perceptions of African Americans were not only created through literature and music— they were visual, too. He wanted African Americans to be proud of themselves, their color, and their features—and to stop trying to be like whites. "Let us train ourselves to see beauty in 'black,'" he said.[3]

Breaking the Molds

One of the first African-American artists to begin breaking out of the old ways was Meta Warrick Fuller, a sculptor. She began studying art in the United States and continued her training in Paris. There, she met the famous sculptor Auguste Rodin, who told her "You are a sculptor. You have the sense of flow in your fingers."[4] While studying with Rodin, Fuller met DuBois, who was visiting Paris. When DuBois saw her work, he encouraged Fuller to start using African themes. She took his advice.

Fuller's most famous work is *Ethiopia Awakening*. It is a bronze life-size sculpture of a woman wearing an Egyptian headdress whose lower body is encased in mummy wrappings. This sculpture, a symbol of the birth of the New Negro, first appeared publicly in New York City for the *Making of America* exhibit. Fuller set an excellent example of portraying African Americans as strong and beautiful. Her work inspired other sculptors, including Augusta Savage, Richmond Barthe, and Sargent Johnson.

Harlem Renaissance painters were also portraying African Americans in new ways. When Aaron Douglas first came to Harlem, his paintings were very traditional. European painter Winold Reiss encouraged Douglas to try using African and modern art styles

James Van Der Zee

James Van Der Zee began taking photographs when he received a camera for his fourteenth birthday. He moved from Lenox, Massachusetts, to New York City when he was 19 and worked as an elevator operator. At age 25, he got a job in a photography studio as a darkroom assistant and quickly rose to the position of photographer. A few years later, he opened his own studio next door to the Harlem Public Library and soon became a popular portrait photographer.

Van Der Zee often posed his subjects in front of romantic-looking backdrops he had painted himself, such as a pool in the moonlight, a French garden scene, or a fire in a hearth. He also did elegant wedding and funeral photography, often retouching the photographs to make his subjects look more glamorous, which customers loved.

Famous Harlem citizens such as Walker, Cullen, Garvey, and many others came to Van Der Zee for portraits. Although he worked mainly in the studio, Van Der Zee also photographed images of street life in Harlem. In all his work, Van Der Zee was committed to the Harlem Renaissance values of uplifting the race and portraying African Americans with dignity.

in new ways. Douglas created a distinctive style that fused African art, cubism (a technique that uses flat geometric shapes), and abstract forms.

Archibald Motley was another painter who changed his focus from European to African-American subject matter. Motley would not depict African Americans in servant roles but created warm portraits of them that emphasize their dignity. Motley hoped this would change negative ideas about African Americans. In 1927, at the height of the Harlem Renaissance, Motley had a successful solo exhibition of his work in New York City. Afterward, he traveled in the South painting people and landscapes. He then won a Guggenheim Fellowship and studied in Paris for one year. His most famous painting, *Blues*, was inspired by a jazz nightclub in Paris.

For some artists, the New Negro ideal set them free to express themselves in new ways. But the ideal seemed to push others into corners. Like Douglas, Motley, and other painters, William H. Johnson began painting in traditional academic styles. But after studying modern artists such as Vincent Van Gogh, he began experimenting with expressionism. Expressionism was a modern style that used bright colors and broad strokes. Many New Negro critics frowned upon Johnson's work. They claimed his new technique was too primitive. Painting in this style did not uplift the New Negro ideal, they said. They felt it reinforced negative racial stereotypes of African Americans as crude and uneducated. However, many artists hailed his work. The Harmon Foundation even awarded him a gold medal for his painting *Jacobia Hotel*.

Although the artists of the Harlem Renaissance did not receive as much attention from the public as the writers and musicians received, they took the first steps toward developing African-American art for future generations. They were the first to begin making images of African Americans as strong, beautiful, and dignified. Their works of truth and beauty have enriched not only African-American culture, but all of US culture as well. ⌐

The Harmon Foundation

The Harmon Foundation was established in Harlem in 1922 by a white real-estate tycoon named William Harmon. The Harmon Foundation developed city playgrounds, gave loans to underprivileged students, and encouraged the expansion of African-American art. Many unknown African-American artists garnered recognition for their talent because of the Harmon Foundation's efforts to give a forum to people who were overlooked by the white art establishment. Financial difficulties caused by the Great Depression forced the foundation to stop giving financial awards and sponsoring art exhibits, but it continued to work to educate the public about the importance of African-American art.

Street Musicians, *a work of art by William H. Johnson*

Chapter
8

Florence Mills became popular after her role in Shuffle Along.

THE MUSIC
AND THE MUSICIANS

hile others were defining the ideas and images of the Harlem Renaissance, the musicians were defining its sound. In fact, it was the music that made the Harlem Renaissance so famous. During the 1920s, African-American musicians from all over the United States began bringing together the music from various regions. They were creating new styles of music and ways of playing. From spirituals, ragtime, and blues came jazz, and from jazz came swing.

Many historians mark the beginning of the Harlem Renaissance with the 1921 opening of the Broadway musical *Shuffle Along*, which featured an all African-American cast. Composed by the writing duo of Eubie Blake and Noble Sissle, *Shuffle Along* became a Broadway smash hit nearly overnight. The success of this musical opened opportunities for more black performers.

AFRICAN-AMERICAN MUSIC HISTORY

The earliest documented music created by African Americans, and recognized by mainstream white society, was the spiritual. Spirituals grew out of the music that enslaved

Florence Mills

Florence Mills became an instant star in the 1921 musical *Shuffle Along*. She was dainty and graceful, singing and moving beautifully. Mills often brought her audience to tears with her song "I'm a Little Blackbird Looking for a Bluebird." One critic said, "She owns the house—no audience in the world can resist that. . . . [She] controlled the emotions of the audience as only a true artist can . . . there was a heart-throb in her bird-like voice . . . all natural art."[1] Tragically, Mills died of appendicitis in 1927 at age 32. Thousands mourned her. At her funeral, a chorus of 500 sang accompanied by a 200-piece orchestra.

Africans had brought from their homelands. White slaveholders did not allow slaves to speak or sing in their native languages, so slaves adapted the basic forms of Europeans hymns, which they were allowed to sing. They infused them with African sounds, rhythms, and singing styles. Since many plantation owners did not allow their slaves to dance, spirituals often incorporated hand clapping, foot tapping, and swaying to music with arms upraised.

During the Harlem Renaissance, several black college choirs, such as the Fisk Jubilee Singers from Fisk University in Nashville, Tennessee, toured the United States and Europe singing these Negro spirituals. But some New Negro critics disapproved. They thought these songs romanticized slavery. It was demeaning for modern black singers to perform slave music for white audiences because it reminded critics of the days when white slave owners forced their slaves to entertain them by singing spirituals. It was fine for African Americans to sing spirituals among themselves but not to perform for whites. Other African Americans felt performing spirituals was a way to honor their heritage. It was also a way to remind the world what white people had done and how black people had endured.

Blues grew out of the work songs sung by the southern slaves who had come from West Africa. While they worked in the fields, black slaves created a call-and-response form of singing they called field hollers. They sang field hollers in a strong rhythmic style to help them keep up their spirits and work together in all kinds of backbreaking labor. Over the years, African Americans developed blues music by essentially taking the spirit of the field hollers and adding melodies and structure. Blues music also inspired the artists whose poems, stories, and paintings came out of the Harlem Renaissance.

RAGTIME AND STRIDE PIANO

Ragtime was a fast musical style that became a craze in the United States during the 1890s. Scott Joplin, who became known as the "King of Ragtime," was an African-American pianist who popularized and elevated

Ethel Waters

Ethel Waters was born in a slum. Growing up, she often stole food to survive. At the age of 13, she married an abusive 23-year-old man but left him a year later. Waters later said, "I was never a child. I never felt I belonged."[2]

In the early 1920s, she began singing in Edmonds's Cellar, a Harlem honky-tonk saloon where she became popular for her peculiar singing and dancing. After recording two songs for the newly formed Black Swan record label, she became a star and one of the most successful African-American entertainers during the Harlem Renaissance and beyond.

Joplin was one of the first popular ragtime musicians.

this style.[3] Though he did not live to see ragtime accepted as a musical art form, Joplin's ragtime compositions were wildly popular for several years.

Around 1920, ragtime piano music starting losing its popularity as blues became the latest craze. But Harlem ragtime pianists—always quick to adapt to changes and try something new—started experimenting with different sounds and styles. That is how they created the stride piano style. According to Nick Morrison, who researched stride piano history for National Public Radio,

> Stride pianists took the basic left-hand 'oompah' rhythm of ragtime, but played it with more swing and complexity, while the right hand played the melody and the ever-increasing improvisations upon it. As the left-hand bass-playing became more complex . . . the pianist's left hand had to literally 'stride' up and down the keyboard—often at great speed.[4]

Harlem's most famous stride pianist was Fats Waller. By the time he was 18, Waller had recorded several songs and was popular in

Black Swan

In the 1900s, whites dominated the recording industry. Although white producers used African-American music, they seldom allowed blacks to make records. Harry Herbert Pace, a student of DuBois, wanted to change this. Pace explained, "Companies would not entertain any thought of recording a colored musician or colored voice, I therefore decided to form my own company and make such recordings as I believed would sell."[5] Pace started a Harlem recording company using the label Black Swan, and its records of Ethel Waters's blues singing were a hit. Unfortunately, Black Swan was unable to survive. It folded in 1924.

Harlem. Throughout the 1920s, Waller composed songs for Fletcher Henderson's orchestra and cowrote for the musical *Keep Shufflin'* in 1928. In 1929, he composed the score for the Broadway musical *Hot Chocolates*, which introduced his famous song "Ain't Misbehavin'."

EARLY JAZZ

Jazz music began in New Orleans, Louisiana, around 1900 before moving into Harlem. What made it different was the way several musicians at once would begin improvising in the middle of a song. Formal European music had always relied on musicians playing sheet music and following a conductor. But many jazz musicians did not read music, so they made up the music as they went along. They might start by playing a popular song, but when they were done, the song would be something completely different.

Joe "King" Oliver

Joe "King" Oliver is one of the most important early jazz musicians. His hot jazz style, also known as Dixieland music, "got its name from its blazing tempos and fiery improvisations."[6] Hot jazz bands usually feature trumpet, trombone, clarinet, tuba, banjo, and drums.

Oliver was famous for putting all kinds of objects in the bell of his trumpet to create unusual sounds. One of his colleagues called him a "freak trumpeter" because he used derby hats, bottles, cups, glasses, and buckets as well as mutes and kazoos.[7] Oliver was blind in one eye and often played his trumpet with a hat tilted over his bad eye.

Trumpeter Louis Armstrong was the most famous New Orleans jazz artist to bring his music to Harlem. He was also among the first jazz musicians to make records. He joined Fletcher Henderson's band at the Roseland Ballroom in New York City. These artists were partially responsible for developing a new style of jazz called swing, fun, quick-tempo dance music. Armstrong also made many recordings with Fletcher during this time, playing cornet and trumpet.

Duke Ellington

Edward Kennedy Ellington was born in 1899 to a middle-class family in Washington DC. His mother adored him and he grew up very confident in himself. His elegant clothing and manners earned him the nickname Duke when he was a teenager.

Ellington began playing the piano in childhood but did not take formal lessons. Instead, he learned from watching and listening to other successful piano players and copied their styles. As a teenager, he and some of his friends formed a band. They took their band to New York in 1923 and soon became popular playing in various nightclubs. Ellington once described his musical inspiration and his race:

My men and my race are the inspiration of my work. I try to catch the character and mood and feeling of my people. The music of my race is something more. . . . It is the result of our transplantation to the American soil, and was our reaction, in plantation days, to the life we lived. What we could not say openly we expressed in music. The characteristic, melancholic music of my race has been forged from the white heat of our sorrows and from our groping.[8]

The Big Band Sound

In 1927, Duke Ellington and his band became the house band at the Cotton Club. There, he added more musicians to create an impressive jazz orchestra and the big band sound that would be popular for decades. Duke Ellington and the Cotton Club Orchestra became famous through weekly radio broadcasts that were heard all over the country. This brought even more attention to Harlem. Ellington's work blended African-American forms of spirituals, ragtime, blues, and jazz with classical European styles and forms.

One of the main reasons the Harlem Renaissance is remembered so well today is because of the power of African-American music. African Americans' innovative musical efforts during the Harlem Renaissance enriched the music of the nation and permanently changed the course of composition and the performing arts. ⌐

Duke Ellington, front, with his Cotton Club Orchestra

*Crowds in Manhattan, New York City,
panic after the stock market crashes on October 29, 1929.*

THE END OF THE RENAISSANCE

istorians have different ideas about
when and why the Harlem Renaissance
ended. Some say the financial collapse of Wall Street
that marked the beginning of the Great Depression
had a devastating impact on Harlem. Others say the

Harlem Renaissance period continued throughout the Depression and ended when World War II (1939–1945) began. But some believe the Harlem Renaissance never died—it merely evolved as times changed and is still alive today.

THE STOCK MARKET CRASH

When the US stock market crashed on October 29, 1929, the United States experienced an economic collapse that plunged the nation into poverty. During the course of the next decade, millions lost their jobs, their savings, their businesses, and their homes. Cars stood rusting in the streets because people did not have money for gas. Shops and businesses were boarded up. Hardworking people who once had secure jobs were out of work and facing starvation. They had no money to buy food and had to stand in long lines to get free bread from the government.

During the 1920s, Saturday nights in Harlem had meant that hundreds of white people in fancy clothes would be spending money freely in clubs, stores, and restaurants. But in the 1930s, many white people turned away from Harlem. They were too concerned with their own problems. For many white people, the interest in Harlem and its people was just a phase. It was something they grew tired of because it was no longer new and exciting.

As the nation sank into the Great Depression, it hurt most everyone in the United States—but it hit African Americans even harder. Many lost their homes. The amount of property owned or managed by African Americans fell from 30 percent in 1932 to 5 percent in 1935. In Harlem, unemployment was five times higher than in the rest of New York City. The few jobs that were available outside of Harlem almost always went to white men. When it came to finding

---

Poverty during the Great Depression

The threat of starvation was very real during the Depression. People foraged for food in garbage cans and city dumps and fought over the scraps. Jobless men robbed trucks delivering food to hotels and grocery stores.

Churches and charities organized soup kitchens and breadlines to help ease the suffering. In the mornings, long lines of hungry people wound down sidewalks for several blocks waiting for small handouts of bread or soup. Those who could not feed their children often sent them out to beg or steal whatever they could. Others panhandled on the streets or begged from door to door from those who still had places to live.

Many people lost their homes because they could not afford to pay their rent or mortgages. Homeless people slept wherever they could—park benches, doorways, under bushes and bridges, vacated buildings, empty boxcars, and abandoned automobiles. On the edges of towns, people built little shelters out of scraps of metal, wood, and cardboard.

work from white employers, black men had always
been the last hired and first fired. Now equality
looked further away than ever. Racial resentment and
suspicion began growing. Still, African Americans
kept moving into Harlem from other parts of
the country. This combination of poverty and
overcrowding eventually turned the black mecca into
a city slum.

HARLEM LEADERS DISPERSE

As Harlem declined, the former New Negro
leaders sought work elsewhere. Fisk University in
Nashville, Tennessee, attracted several. Charles S.
Johnson, coordinator of the Civic Club dinner and
contributor to New Negro thought, became Fisk's
director of social sciences. James Weldon Johnson,
Opportunity's original editor, moved to Fisk to teach
English in 1931. The great artist Aaron Douglas
arrived at Fisk in 1937 where he taught for nearly
20 years. Locke focused his attentions on his work
at Howard University, where his philosophies would
influence the next generations of students.

DuBois struggled to keep the *Crisis* magazine
alive, even giving up his salary to pay for printing
costs. After 1934, DuBois no longer edited the *Crisis*.

Unemployed New Yorkers wait in line for government assistance.

Jessie Fauset, DuBois's closest associate at the magazine, quit her job there to marry and become a housewife. Her last novel was published in 1933.

FRIENDSHIPS LOST

The end of the Harlem Renaissance also brought the breakup of several important friendships and collaborations. Locke's two favorite protégés, Hughes and Hurston, were writing a play together called *Mule Bone*. They wanted to combine Hurston's research on African-American folklore with Hughes's lyrical writing style and start an authentic Negro theater company. They were excited and hopeful about their project—and so was Godmother Mason. She provided them a quiet house in which to live and work. She even hired a typist to make it easier for them to produce something great. But Locke thought they were not doing their best. He told Mason the two writers were spending more time partying than writing. Hurston, jealous of Hughes's friendship with their female typist, took a sudden trip to the South. And Hughes had to answer to Mason alone. He was humiliated by the encounter but did not know that Locke had undermined him and Hurston. Though he tried for months to get back into Mason's good graces, she never helped him again.

Hurston finished the *Mule Bone* script alone and then copyrighted it under her name, denying Hughes's part in its creation. This caused a rift among other Harlemites, many of whom ended up taking Hughes's side and shunning Hurston. Mason eventually sent Hurston away as well, leaving Locke as her sole remaining godchild from the Harlem Renaissance. Hughes never reconciled with Hurston or Locke.

DEATH OF THE RENAISSANCE?

DuBois believed the Harlem Renaissance did not last because it was created for a white audience. It was a reaction to white racism that depended on white sympathy and support. Many others agreed. Hughes said, "How could a large and enthusiastic number of people be crazy about Negroes forever?"[1] And McKay said it "was really inspired and kept alive by the interest and presence of [whites]. It faded out when they became tired of the new plaything."[2]

But perhaps DuBois was only partially correct. Some contributors

"Harlem, physically at least, has changed very little in my parents' lifetime or in mine. Now as then the buildings are old and in desperate need of repair, the streets are crowded and dirty, there are too many human beings per square block. . . . All over Harlem now there is felt the same bitter expectancy with which, in my childhood, we awaited winter: it is coming and it will be hard, there is nothing anyone can do about it. All of Harlem is pervaded by a sense of congestion . . . like . . . trying to breathe in a very small room with all the windows shut."[3]
—James Baldwin, 1948

to the Harlem Renaissance thrived during the Depression and afterward. Hurston did her best work in the 1930s, including her collection of folklore titled *Mules and Men* and *Their Eyes Were Watching God*. Musicians and performers such as Duke Ellington and Ethel Waters also did well. More African-American performers found work in film. Still others found refuge in teaching and in passing on their knowledge to a new generation.

A New Renaissance

Many modern writers, musicians, artists, and performers were first inspired by works of those in the Harlem Renaissance. Douglas's murals still grace the walls of the 135th Street Library in Harlem, a proud statement to people today. Hurston's writing alone has inspired many successful authors, including Alice Walker, Ralph Ellison, Toni Morrison, and Gayle Jones. Martin Luther King Jr. and Malcolm X were influenced by the lives and philosophies of those who led the Harlem Renaissance—and the civil rights and Black Power movements of the 1960s were like a new Harlem Renaissance. Some people today are comparing hip-hop culture to the Harlem Renaissance because it has

Alice Walker

Alice Walker, author of the Pulitzer Prize–winning novel *The Color Purple*, discovered the writings of Hurston when she was a college student in the 1970s. In an interview with National Public Radio, Walker discussed Hurston's belief in the importance of trusting one's own reality: "Without a foundation in our own reality . . . people don't know what to do. . . . They don't know what to buy, they don't know what kind of house to live in. . . they don't know who they are. For god's sake and for goddesses' sake . . . appreciate who you are. There is nobody finer on this planet for you to emulate than yourself."[4]

its own music, literature, graffiti art, fashion, and slang terms.

Now more than ever before, people are recognizing the greatness of African-American contributions to US society. The spirit of the Harlem Renaissance lives when people recognize the beauty of their heritage and cherish their own identity, follow their own creative dreams, speak out for those who have no voice, and work for equality for all.

*The Harlem Renaissance helped pave the way
for the civil rights movement.*

TIMELINE

1658	1664	1909
The Dutch settle Nieuw Haarlem in the New Netherland territory, which is present-day Manhattan.	After taking over the territory from the Dutch, the British give locations new names: Harlem, New York City, and New York.	The NAACP is founded.

1921	1921	1922
The Broadway musical *Shuffle Along* opens on May 23. Many consider this the official start of the Harlem Renaissance.	The *Crisis* publishes Langston Hughes's poem "The Negro Speaks of Rivers" in June.	Claude McKay publishes his volume of poetry titled *Harlem Shadows*.

1910	1919	1920
The National Urban League is founded.	Following World War I, the 369th Infantry, an all-black unit of soldiers, march into Harlem amid cheering crowds on February 17.	Blues music starts to become popular.

1923	1923	1924
After discovering his African-American roots, Jean Toomer publishes *Cane*.	The Cotton Club opens in the fall.	On March 21, *Opportunity* magazine's Civic Club dinner introduces prominent white publishers to black writers.

TIMELINE

1924	1925	1925
In November, Countee Cullen's poems are published in *Harper's* magazine.	James Weldon Johnson publishes *The Book of American Negro Spirituals* to allow others to explore the African-American culture.	On March 1, *Survey Graphic* publishes a special edition that focuses on African-American creative artists and writers.

1927	1927	1927
Archibald Motley has a successful exhibition of his artwork that depicts African Americans with dignity.	Duke Ellington and his band become the house band at the Cotton Club.	Charlotte Mason becomes Godmother to Hughes and Zora Neale Hurston, paying them to pursue their writing and research.

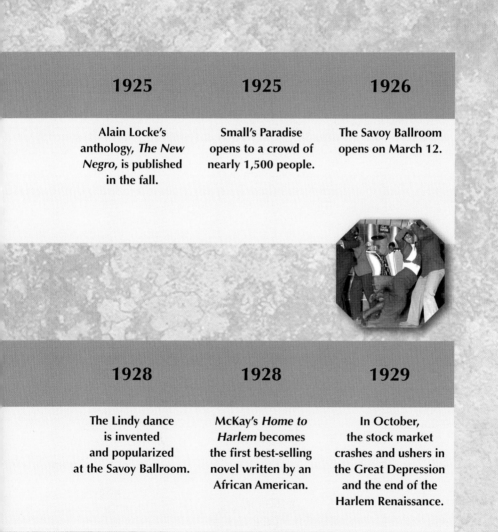

1925

Alain Locke's anthology, *The New Negro*, is published in the fall.

1925

Small's Paradise opens to a crowd of nearly 1,500 people.

1926

The Savoy Ballroom opens on March 12.

1928

The Lindy dance is invented and popularized at the Savoy Ballroom.

1928

McKay's *Home to Harlem* becomes the first best-selling novel written by an African American.

1929

In October, the stock market crashes and ushers in the Great Depression and the end of the Harlem Renaissance.

Essential Facts

Date of Event

Approximately 1919 to 1930

Place of Event

The Harlem neighborhood of Manhattan in New York City. The cultural phenomenon of the Harlem Renaissance also influenced African-American communities throughout the United States and Europe.

Key Players

- Louis Armstrong
- Aaron Douglas
- W. E. B. DuBois
- Duke Ellington
- Marcus Garvey
- Langston Hughes
- Zora Neale Hurston
- Alain Locke
- Claude McKay
- James Weldon Johnson

Highlights of Event

❖ Returning World War I heroes, the Harlem Hellfighters, marched through New York City on February 17, 1919.

❖ Eubie Blake and Noble Sissle's musical revue *Shuffle Along* opened on Broadway in 1921 and became a smash hit.

❖ On March 21, 1924, *Opportunity* magazine hosted the Civic Club dinner, which helped Harlem Renaissance writers connect with white publishers.

❖ In 1925, Alain Locke published *The New Negro*, a critically acclaimed collection of stories, poems, and essays by Harlem Renaissance writers such as Countee Cullen, Langston Hughes, Claude McKay, W. E. B. DuBois, and James Weldon Johnson. It also features art by Aaron Douglas.

❖ The Savoy Ballroom opened in 1926. Many new dances were invented and popularized at the Savoy, including the famous Lindy.

❖ The Cotton Club hired Duke Ellington's band in 1927. Nationwide radio broadcasts of Ellington's music made him a household name.

❖ In 1928, Claude McKay's *Home to Harlem* was published and became the first best-selling novel by an African-American author.

Quote

"The music of my race is . . . the result of our transplantation to the American soil, and it was our reaction to plantation days, to the life we lived. What we could not say openly we expressed in music. The characteristic, melancholic music of my race has been forged from the very white heat of our sorrow."—*Duke Ellington*

GLOSSARY

anthropology
> The study of humans and culture.

apogee
> The highest point.

cabaret
> A restaurant that provides entertainment such as music and dancing.

capitalize
> To take advantage of something in order to make money from it.

deference
> Respectful submission.

etiquette
> An accepted code of behavior.

influx
> The entry or coming in of something.

mecca
> A place where many people want to visit.

melancholic
> Sad, sorrowful.

perpetuate
> To keep something going.

prolific
> Very productive.

protégé
> A person under the care or protection of someone who is interested in his or her career or welfare.

segregation
> The separation of a certain group, often a race, from the rest of society.

speculator
> Someone who engages in risky business deals in order to make large profits.

supremacist
> A person who believes his or her race or group is superior to others.

syncopation
> A musical rhythm that stresses the unaccented beats, as in some West African rhythms.

vernacular
> The everyday language of a culture.

ADDITIONAL RESOURCES

SELECTED BIBLIOGRAPHY

Boyd, Valerie. *Wrapped in Rainbows: The Life of Zora Neale Hurston*. New York: Scribner, 2003. Print.

Gates, Henry Louis, Jr., and Evelyn Brooks Higginbotham, eds. *Harlem Renaissance Lives*. New York: Oxford UP, 2009. Print.

Honey, Maureen, ed. *Shadowed Dreams: Women's Poetry of the Harlem Renaissance*. New Brunswick, NJ: Rutgers UP, 2006. Print.

Watson, Steven. *The Harlem Renaissance: Hub of African-American Culture 1920–1930*. New York: Pantheon, 1995. Print.

FURTHER READINGS

Abdul-Jabbar, Kareem. *On the Shoulders of Giants: My Journey through the Harlem Renaissance*. New York: Simon, 2007. Print.

Hill, Laban Carrick. *Harlem Stomp!: A Cultural History of the Harlem Renaissance*. New York: Little, 2003. Print.

Howes, Kelly King. *Harlem Renaissance*. Boston: Gale, 2001. Print.

Web Links

To learn more about the Harlem Renaissance, visit ABDO Publishing Company online at **www.abdopublishing.com**. Web sites about the Harlem Renaissance are featured on our Book Links page. These links are routinely monitored and updated to provide the most current information available.

Places to Visit

Harlem Heritage Tourism & Cultural Center
104 Malcolm X Boulevard, New York, NY 10026
212-280-7888
http://www.harlemheritage.com
Harlem Heritage Tourism & Cultural Center offers bus and walking tours of the Harlem area. Tour guides are native Harlemites.

The Studio Museum in Harlem
144 West 125th Street, New York, NY 10027
212-864-4500
http://www.studiomuseum.org
The Studio Museum in Harlem displays and promotes African-American visual art.

Source Notes

Chapter 1. The Two Harlems
1. Langston Hughes. *The Big Sea*. Columbia: U of Missouri P, 2002. Print. 176.
2. Marshall Stearns and Jean Stearns. *Jazz Dance: The Story of American Vernacular Dance*. New York: Da Capo, 1994. Print. 316.
3. Kareem Abdul-Jabbar. *On the Shoulders of Giants: My Journey Through the Harlem Renaissance*. New York: Simon and Schuster, 2007. Print. 37.

Chapter 2. From Haarlem to Harlem
1. Henry Louis Gates, Jr. and Evelyn Brooks Higgenbotham. *Harlem Renaissance Lives*. New York: Oxford UP, 2009. Print. 395.

Chapter 3. Black Mecca
1. "Zora Neale Hurston's Glossary of Harlem Slang." *aalbc.com*. aalbc.com, 2011. Web. 10 Mar. 2011.
2. Philip Dray. *At the Hands of Persons Unknown: The Lynching of Black America*. New York: Modern Library, 2002. Print. 237.
3. James Weldon Johnson. *Black Manhattan*. New York: Da Capo, 1991. Print. 163.

Chapter 4. The New Negro Movement
1. W. E. B. DuBois. *The Souls of Black Folk*. New York: Dover, 1994. Print. xxxiv.
2. Steven Watson. *The Harlem Renaissance: Hub of African-American Culture 1920–1930*. New York: Pantheon, 1995. Print. 25.
3. G. Reginald Daniel. *Race and Multiraciality in Brazil and the United States: Converging Paths?* Philadelphia: Pennsylvania State UP, 2006. Print. 115.
4. "James Reese Europe." *The New Grove Dictionary of Jazz*. Oxford UP, n.d. Web. 10 Mar. 2011.

Chapter 5. Introducing the Writers

1. Steven Watson. *The Harlem Renaissance: Hub of African-American Culture 1920–1930*. New York: Pantheon, 1995. Print. 27.

2. Henry Louis Gates, Jr. and Evelyn Brooks Higginbotham. *Harlem Renaissance Lives*. New York: Oxford UP, 2009. Print. 134.

3. Steven Watson. *The Harlem Renaissance: Hub of African-American Culture 1920–1930*. New York: Pantheon, 1995. Print. 28.

4. Ibid. 42.

5. Ibid. 47.

6. Ibid. 29.

7. Henry Louis Gates, Jr. and Evelyn Brooks Higginbotham. *Harlem Renaissance Lives*. New York: Oxford UP, 2009. Print. 343.

Chapter 6. Diversity and Disagreement

1. Deborah G. Plant. *Zora Neale Hurston: A Biography of the Spirit*. Westport, CT: Praeger, 2007. Print. 14.

2. Henry Louis Gates, Jr. and Evelyn Brooks Higginbotham. *Harlem Renaissance Lives*. New York: Oxford UP, 2009. Print. 134–135.

3. Ibid. 273.

4. Steven Watson. *The Harlem Renaissance: Hub of African-American Culture 1920–1930*. New York: Pantheon, 1995. Print. 9.

5. Henry Louis Gates, Jr. and Evelyn Brooks Higginbotham. *Harlem Renaissance Lives*. New York: Oxford UP, 2009. Print. 500.

Chapter 7. The Arts and the Artists

1. Henry Louis Gates, Jr. and Evelyn Brooks Higginbotham. *Harlem Renaissance Lives*. New York: Oxford UP, 2009. Print. 435.

2. Ibid. 212.

3. Manning Marable. *Black Leadership*. New York: Columbia UP, 1998. Print. 46.

4. Henry Louis Gates, Jr. and Evelyn Brooks Higginbotham. *Harlem Renaissance Lives*. New York: Oxford UP, 2009. Print. 161.

Source Notes Continued

Chapter 8. The Music and the Musicians

1. Henry Louis Gates, Jr. and Evelyn Brooks Higginbotham. *Harlem Renaissance Lives*. New York: Oxford UP, 2009. Print. 355.

2. Ibid. 517.

3. Ibid. 314.

4. Nick Morrison. "Stride Piano: Bottom-End Jazz." *National Public Radio: Music*. National Public Radio, 12 Apr. 2010. Web. 10 Mar. 2011.

5. Jitu K. Weusi. "The Rise and Fall of Black Swan Records." *The Red Hot Jazz Archive*. N.p., n.d. Web. 10 Mar. 2011.

6. Jacob Teichroew. "Hot Jazz." *About.com*. New York Times Company, 2011. Web. 10 Mar. 2011.

7. "Oliver King Biography." *Index of Musician Biographies*. Net Industries, 2011. Web. 10 Mar. 2011.

8. Robert E. Johnson. "On His 96th Birthday Duke Ellington Is Proclaimed 'Beyond Category' By Critics of His Great Music." *Jet*. 15 May. 1995. Print. 60.

Chapter 9. The End of the Renaissance

1. Steven Watson. *The Harlem Renaissance: Hub of African-American Culture 1920–1930*. New York: Pantheon, 1995. Print. 159.

2. Ibid. 160.

3. James Baldwin. *Notes of a Native Son*. Boston: Beacon, 1984. Print. 57.

4. Vertamae Grosvenor. "Intersections: Crafting a Voice for Black Culture Alice Walker on Zora Neale Hurston's 'Spiritual Food.'" *National Public Radio*. National Public Radio, 26 Apr. 2004. Web. 10 Mar. 2011.

INDEX

Index Continued

ABOUT THE AUTHOR

DeAnn Herringshaw has been working as a writer, editor, and writing consultant for educational and nonprofit organizations for more than 15 years. She especially enjoys doing research because she loves the challenge of learning and sharing new ideas. She lives in Minnesota.

PHOTO CREDITS